In the beginning ....

Sir Hans Sloane was a great collector. He filled his house with rare books and pictures, fossils and precious stones, stuffed animals, birds and butterflies, and ancient remains from all over the world. There had never been a collection quite like it, and visitors were amazed by what they saw.

When Sir Hans Sloane died in 1753, his will let the King buy the whole collection for just £20,000 so that it could belong to the nation for ever. This was the start of the British Museum. Trustees were put in charge of the collection and they set about finding a home for it. They looked at Buckingham House (now Buckingham Palace) but it was too expensive. In the end they bought Montagu House in Bloomsbury.

The British Museum has been there ever since, growing bigger and bigger ....

It was not long before space ran out in Montagu House. New rooms were added, and finally what was left of the old house was pulled down to make way for a grand new building. It took thirty years and thousands of tons of stone to complete the building and the forty-four massive columns which decorate the front.

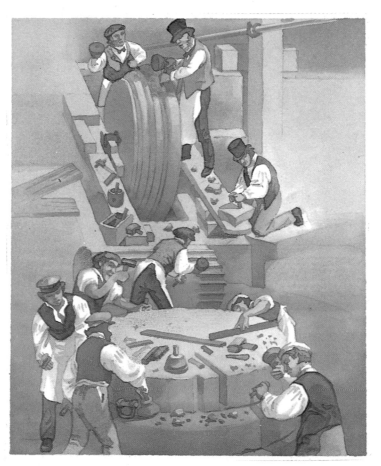

The building was finished in 1848, but the museum collections have gone on growing, and the work of repairing, reorganising and enlarging never stops.

Montagu House
was here

From animals to antiquities...

The British Museum started as a museum which collected everything. At first it was particularly famous for its natural history collection and its vast library of books.

Three stuffed giraffes used to stand at the top of the stairs in old Montagu house.

In the 1880s all the museum's stuffed animals and birds and pickled specimens were moved to the new Natural History museum at South Kensington.

Children today are sometimes surprised not to find any dinosaurs in the museum ... but there are plenty of other ancient and marvellous things to look at.

The museum's huge collection of books and manuscripts has now become the British Library. Many fine examples of famous books, Bibles, illuminated manuscripts and old maps are displayed in the British Library galleries in the museum.

For over two and a quarter centuries the collections of 'antiquities' have gone on growing. Today the British Museum is a

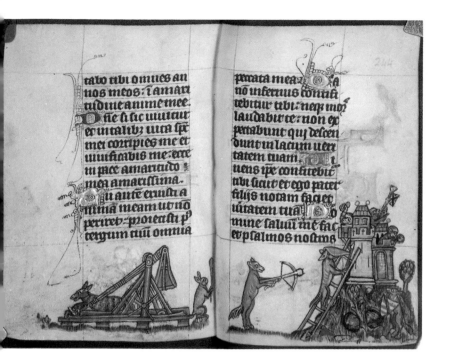

treasure house of old, beautiful and interesting objects. They come from all over the world and from thousands of years of history. The one thing they have in common is that they have all been made by hand. Every exhibit reveals the skill of its maker and tells us something about the time and place in which it was made.

Animals laying siege to a castle decorate the pages of this hand-written book, now in the British Library.

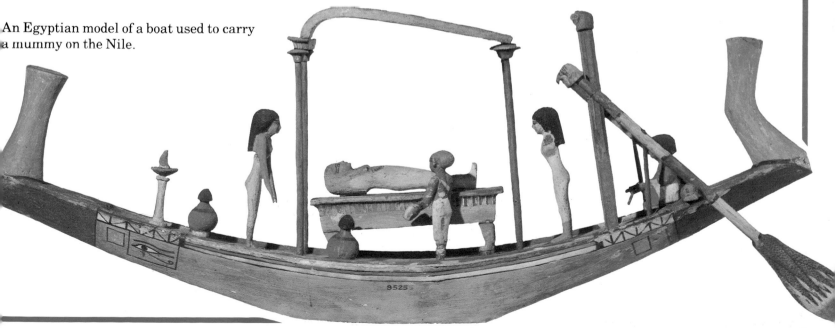

An Egyptian model of a boat used to carry a mummy on the Nile.

Inside information

The museum has about 6,000,000 visitors a year.

The largest number of visitors in one day was 33,000.

The heaviest exhibit is a winged bull made of stone. It weighs 16 tonnes (as much as two double-decker buses)!

The distance round the museum through all the galleries is 2½ miles.

The tallest exhibit is the totem pole which is over 11 metres high.

The oldest exhibits in the museum are stone tools from Africa more than a million years old.

The thousands of things you can see on display are just a small part of the museum's collections, and a lot of work goes on behind the scenes.

Scholars from all over the world come to the British Museum to study. They

can compare one pot (or coin, or flint tool) with a hundred others to work out when and where it was made.

The public galleries contain just the most beautiful and interesting examples.

About a thousand people work in the museum. Here is an introduction to some of them.

The Director...
is in charge of the whole Museum.

Curators...
including the Keepers who are in charge of each department, study and find out about the objects and take good care of them.

Warders...
look after the galleries and keep the museum safe. They help visitors who ask them the way.

Technicians...
locksmiths, painters and carpenters are at work every day making and mending around the museum.

Cleaners...
start work at seven each morning before visitors arrive. There is an area of floor as large as thirteen football pitches to keep clean!

...and museum cats frighten off the mice.

Scientists at work

The British Museum has a laboratory with powerful modern equipment. Scientists carry out detective work there on objects from the museum, and on finds from excavations. They work out the answers to questions like

What is it made of?
How was it made?
How old is it?
Is it a fake?

What is it made of?

What would you think this mirror was made of? Everyone thought it was made of bronze like other Greek and Roman mirrors in the museum. Bronze contains copper and tin, and copper becomes covered with green corrosion like this when it is buried.

Scientists in the laboratory were trying to discover more about the metals used by the Greeks and Romans. When they tested a bit of this mirror they were puzzled because the metal did not behave like bronze.

They then used a special technique for analysing metal and the results said

Silver 92%
Copper 8%

Once they knew what it was made of, it was possible to clean it properly. The British Museum now has a rare Roman silver mirror on display!

How old is it?

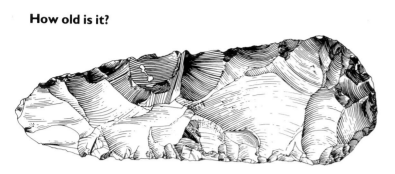

This unfinished tool was shaped by stone-age workmen at the Grime's Graves flint mines in Norfolk.

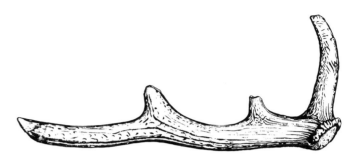

In the holes where flints like this were found there were antlers from large deer which the miners had used as picks to dig out the stone.

Scientists in the British Museum laboratory have worked out how old it is.

Everything which has ever been alive contains a tiny amount of 'radiocarbon'. When this is measured, the length of time since it stopped living can be worked out. You cannot tell the age of stone or metal by radiocarbon dating, but you can discover the age of any wood, charcoal, bone, cloth, leather or seeds found close by.

Samples from an antler pick were put through the equipment in the laboratory and the radiocarbon was measured. By working out the age of the antler the scientists can tell that this flint tool must have been made about four thousand years ago.

Conservators at work

Conservators in the British Museum keep the objects in good condition so that they can be enjoyed now and in the future. Many of the objects which come into the museum need cleaning and mending. Materials such as metal, stone, pottery, paper and cloth all have to be treated in different ways. Conservators also know how to display objects so that they will not tarnish or fade or crack.

The Sophilos Vase is a magnificent Greek pot which needed putting together again.

1. The 118 clay pieces were cleaned, and laid out like a jigsaw puzzle.

2. The pieces were fitted together and glued. The vase was balanced in a tray of sand to keep it steady.

3. Soft wax was pressed on the inside, and slid round under the gaps. The gaps were filled in with plaster of paris.

4. The plaster was tinted to match the vase, but the conservators did not try to paint in all the missing pieces. They want you to be able to see which parts are old and which are new.

Learning to mend pots
With a hammer, break a clay flower-pot (or an old bowl, but not the best dinner plate!) into about ten pieces. Hide away a few small fragments. Cut some short lengths of sellotape. Try to put the pot together again, sticking sellotape across the joins as you fit each piece into place. Conservators practise like this when they are beginning to learn how to mend pots.

? Which pieces of the jigsaw can you see fitted together in this picture? Write down the numbers of the pieces you find and then check them on the inside back cover.

The gap at the top is being filled in with plaster of paris.

Mysterious hieroglyphs

In 1799, French soldiers were fighting for Napoleon in Egypt. While building a new fort at a village called Rosetta they came across this strange black stone slab. It was covered in writing, and the same inscription was repeated three times over; first in hieroglyphs (the picture writing of ancient Egypt), then in demotic (another form of Egyptian writing), and finally in Greek.

It was an exciting discovery. No-one had ever been able to understand hieroglyphs before. Now by translating the Greek part first, the meaning of the hieroglyphs could be worked out.

When the English beat the French in Egypt a few years later, the Rosetta stone was brought back to England and put into the British Museum. Scholars set to work and they soon began to crack the hieroglyphic code.

These are some of the discoveries they made:
Hieroglyphs can be written from right to left or from left to right. You have to start reading from the end the creatures are looking towards.

❓ **Are the hieroglyphs on the Rosetta Stone written from right to left or left to right?**
Answer on inside back cover

The oval rings (called cartouches) always hold a royal name. All the cartouches on the Rosetta stone hold the name of King Ptolemy, written in several different ways.

❓ **How many times does his name appear?**
Answer on inside back cover

Hieroglyphs can be used in two ways. The picture can have a meaning in itself, or it can stand for a sound.

Hieroglyph	picture meaning	sound
▯	stool	P
△	loaf	T
🦁	lion	L

👁️ **Can you find these hieroglyphs in Ptolemy's name?**

King Ramesses II had a list made in one of his temples to show the names of kings of Egypt who had ruled before him. His own names were repeated all along the bottom row.

Here are some of the hieroglyphs which were used to show a king's greatness.

	god		king of Egypt
	living for ever		son of Re (the sun god)

👁️ **Look out for these titles on the Rosetta stone and on the list of kings.**

Giant statues

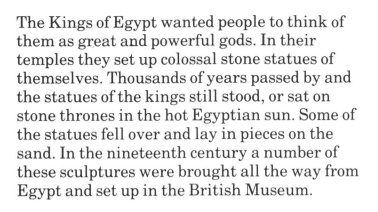

The Kings of Egypt wanted people to think of them as great and powerful gods. In their temples they set up colossal stone statues of themselves. Thousands of years passed by and the statues of the kings still stood, or sat on stone thrones in the hot Egyptian sun. Some of the statues fell over and lay in pieces on the sand. In the nineteenth century a number of these sculptures were brought all the way from Egypt and set up in the British Museum.

If the statue of King Amenophis III were still complete it would be so tall that the head would disappear through the ceiling of the sculpture gallery! The head is nearly three metres tall, and the arm has fingers which are each ten centimetres across.

King Amenophis III was ruling Egypt in 1400 BC. You can meet him several more times in the sculpture gallery.

 Can you see the double crown of Egypt?

The round-topped crown of Upper Egypt sits inside the crown of Lower Egypt on the King's head. The cobra sign on the front is the badge of kingship. Look out for it on the royal statues.

An engineer called Belzoni worked out a way of moving colossal statues. This is how he brought them down to the River Nile to be put onto boats.

On several occasions the Egyptian sculptures have been moved about inside the museum. It is not an easy job. In 1834 army gunners had to move the head of Amenophis III to a new gallery.

👁 **How did they lift it off its base?**

Carved scarab beetles were very popular in ancient Egypt. They were symbols of new life and had magic powers. This is the largest scarab you can see in the museum. It is carved out of black granite.

Egyptian mummies

The Egyptians enjoyed life, and hoped it would carry on in much the same way after death. So it was very important to make sure the spirits of the dead person had a body to live in. Dead bodies soon decay, but the Egyptians found ways of preventing this. At first people were buried in the hot sand, which dried out the bodies and even preserved the skin and hair. Later the problem was solved by making mummies.

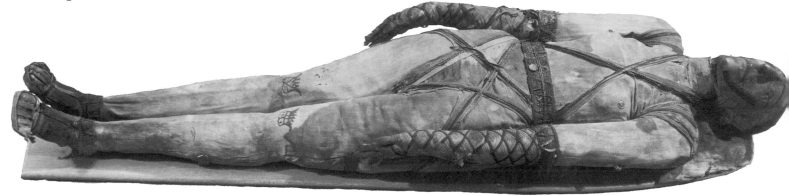

How to make a mummy

1. Cut the body and take out the insides. Treat them and put them into special jars. They will be needed again in the afterlife.
2. Dry the body out by covering it with natron (a form of salt) for forty days.
3. Stuff the body with linen and sawdust to give it a lifelike shape and sew it up again.
4. Anoint the body with scented ointments, and coat it with resin.
5. Wrap the body carefully with up to twenty layers of linen sheeting and long bandages. The right spells must be said while this is being done!

Gods often took the form of an animal, so sacred animals were made into mummies too. You can see mummified birds and cats and even a crocodile in the museum as well as this little bull mummy.

Body-shaped coffins could be made from linen and plaster, or wood, and were put one inside another. This coffin was made for the mummy of a priestess who died about 1000 BC. It was decorated with pictures to help her on her way into the afterlife.

👁 **Can you see?**

gods with animal heads

winged goddesses to protect the body

the sign for life

This shows the special pattern which was painted on rectangular wooden outer coffins. The dead person would be able to see out through the magic eyes and let his spirits come and go through the false doors.

Models and Paintings

The dead were buried with everything they would need in the afterlife, though pictures and models were able to take the place of real things.

These models come from Egyptian tombs. Servants are needed to farm the fields of paradise.

This man is ploughing with oxen.

Someone has to cook the meals. These men are baking bread. One kneads the dough while the other tends the fire.

A 'Book of the Dead' was put into the tomb. It contained magic spells and pictures to guide the dead person through the underworld.

The picture at the top is from a Book of the Dead made for a royal scribe called Hunefer. It shows his mummy being carried on a boat in a procession with servants, cattle, mourners and priests. It was painted on papyrus about 3000 years ago.

Egyptian painters followed a clear set of rules.
When they painted a person they wanted to show as much as possible, so they drew

the head and hair from the side

the eye from in front

the shoulders and chest from in front

the arms according to what the person was doing

the hips from the side

the legs and feet from the side

'see-through' clothes could be added afterwards

Use these rules to help you draw

a servant
a mourner
a priest

Stone lions with wings

In the nineteenth century, archaeologists tried to find out more about places in the Bible which no longer exist. Exciting discoveries were made in the part of the Middle East which used to be Assyria and is now Iraq. Buried a few metres deep under mounds of earth were the remains of mighty palaces. Huge stone monsters still stood at the entrances: enormous lions and bulls with wings like birds and heads like men.

This human-headed winged lion guarded a doorway in the palace of King Ashurnasirpal at Nimrud.

There is something odd about its legs. What is it? Answer on inside back cover

Here it is being pulled up the steps of the British Museum.

The birth of writing

Writing was invented about 5000 years ago in the Middle East where civilisation began. The first writing was called cuneiform and it was used for 3000 years by people including the Sumerians, the Babylonians and the Assyrians.

Cuneiform was usually written on tablets of clay. The end of a reed was cut into a wedge shape and pressed into the damp clay making marks like this

The British Museum has over 100,000 cuneiform tablets. They are very fragile because they were left to harden in the sun but were not fired in a kiln. The museum is now baking the tablets to preserve them, but there are so many that the whole job could take a hundred years.

People could use cylinder seals to sign documents even if they could not write. The pattern was cut into a small cylinder (usually made of stone). When the seal was rolled over wet clay it left its owner's special mark behind.

Sometimes the clay tablets were put into clay envelopes, with the message written again on the outside .... just to make doubly sure!

 Make your own cylinder seal.

Carve out a pattern round a candle stub or chubby wax crayon, using the point of a nail. Roll your cylinder seal over a tablet of clay, plasticine or blu-tack.

Music from the Death Pit

In 1922 the archaeologist Sir Leonard Woolley started excavating the ancient city of Ur in modern Iraq. He found a great cemetery of nearly two thousand graves. In one grave, the Great Death Pit, there were seventy-four skeletons lying in rows. They were probably servants who were killed to go with their master into the afterlife.

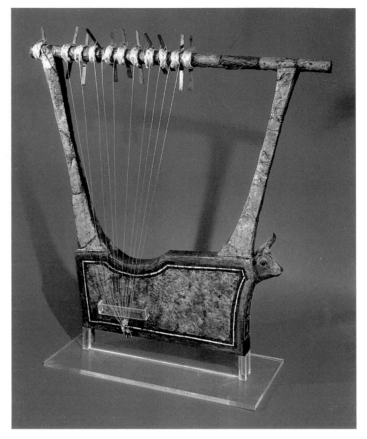

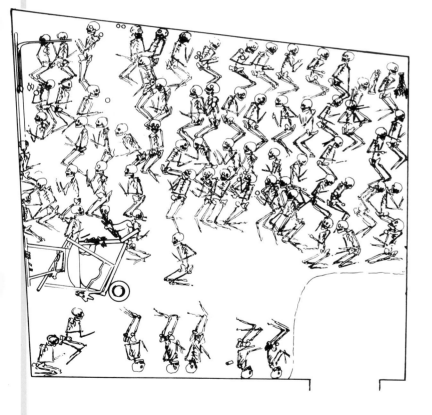

the great death pit

The treasure buried with the servants included this silver lyre. It was squashed flat because the wooden inside had rotted away, leaving only the silver casing.

The lyre is about four and a half thousand years old and the oldest ever found. It has now been restored. Scientists in the laboratory have also made a model of it to discover the sound it made.

A decorated box called the Standard of Ur was found in the great cemetery. It gives a clue to how lyres like this were played.

 Can you see a man playing a bull-headed lyre?

There were three lyres in the Great Death Pit. They were lying in the ground like this.

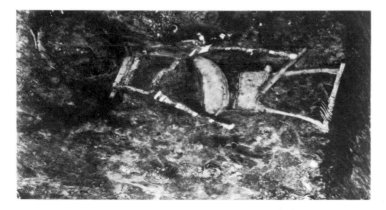

Which is the silver lyre now in the British Museum? Answer on the inside back cover.

Sir Leonard Woolley found more lyres and harps in other tombs. Parts were missing because they had been made of wood, so he did some clever detective work. He poured plaster of Paris into the empty holes to find the exact shape of the missing parts.

Try being an archaeological detective.

Ask a friend to press a small object, such as a clothes peg or a bottle top, into some damp earth and take it out again.

**Put a little water into a container and stir in plaster or Polyfilla powder until it is like thick cream.
Pour this into the hole and leave it to set hard.**

**Ease the plaster cast out of the ground with a knife and brush away any earth.
What clues does it give you about the 'missing object'?**

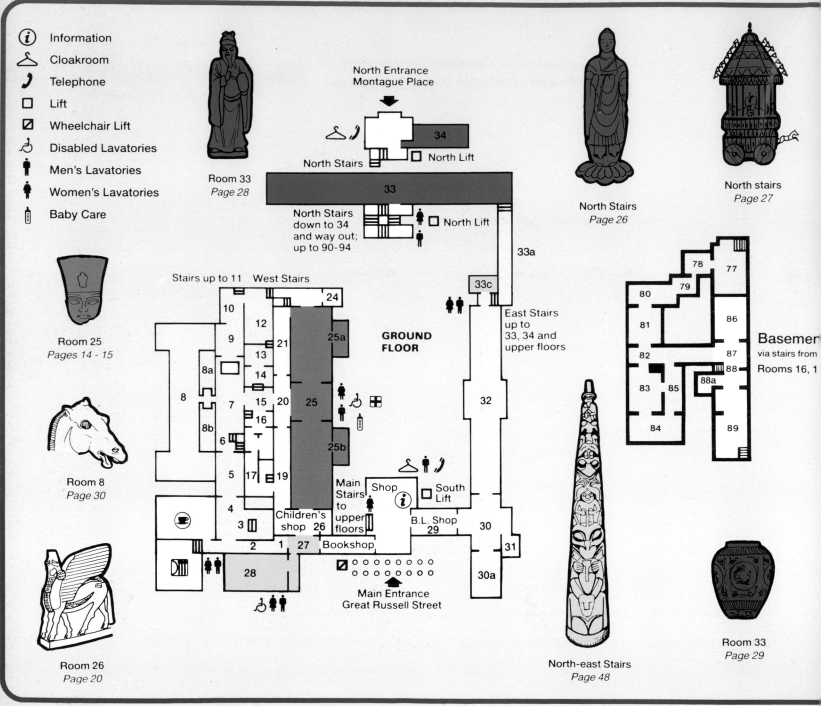

Information ⓘ
Cloakroom
Telephone
Lift
Wheelchair Lift
Disabled Lavatories
Men's Lavatories
Women's Lavatories
Baby Care

Room 33
Page 28

North Stairs
Page 26

North stairs
Page 27

North Entrance
Montague Place

34

North Lift

North Stairs

33

North Stairs
down to 34
and way out;
up to 90-94

North Lift

33a

33c

East Stairs
up to
33, 34 and
upper floors

78
77
79
80
81
86
82
87
88
83 85 88a
84 89

Basemen
via stairs from
Rooms 16, 1

Room 25
Pages 14 - 15

Stairs up to 11   West Stairs

10
12
9
13
21
8a
14
8
7
15 20
8b
16
6
5
17 19
4
3
2 1 27

24
25a

**GROUND
FLOOR**

25

25b

32

Main
Stairs
to
upper
floors

Shop ⓘ

South
Lift

Children's
shop 26

Bookshop

B.L. Shop
29

30

31

30a

28

Main Entrance
Great Russell Street

Room 8
Page 30

Room 26
Page 20

North-east Stairs
Page 48

Room 33
Page 29

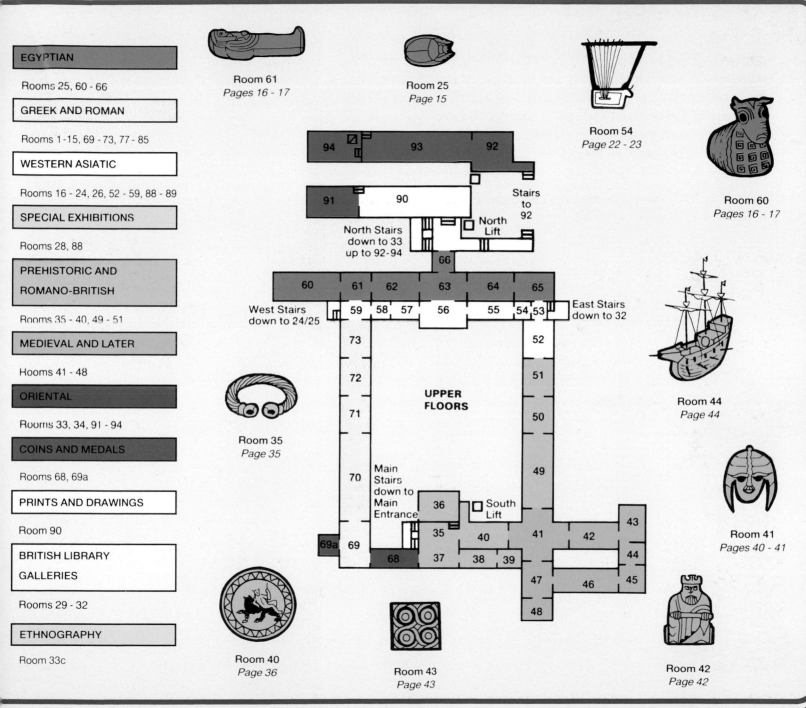

EGYPTIAN

Rooms 25, 60 - 66

GREEK AND ROMAN

Rooms 1-15, 69 - 73, 77 - 85

WESTERN ASIATIC

Rooms 16 - 24, 26, 52 - 59, 88 - 89

SPECIAL EXHIBITIONS

Rooms 28, 88

PREHISTORIC AND
ROMANO-BRITISH

Rooms 35 - 40, 49 - 51

MEDIEVAL AND LATER

Rooms 41 - 48

ORIENTAL

Rooms 33, 34, 91 - 94

COINS AND MEDALS

Rooms 68, 69a

PRINTS AND DRAWINGS

Room 90

BRITISH LIBRARY
GALLERIES

Rooms 29 - 32

ETHNOGRAPHY

Room 33c

Room 61
Pages 16 - 17

Room 25
Page 15

Room 54
Page 22 - 23

Room 60
Pages 16 - 17

Room 35
Page 35

Room 44
Page 44

Room 41
Pages 40 - 41

Room 40
Page 36

Room 43
Page 43

Room 42
Page 42

94 93 92

91 90

Stairs
to
92

North Stairs
down to 33
up to 92-94

North
Lift

66

60 61 62 63 64 65

West Stairs
down to 24/25

59 58 57 56 55 54 53

East Stairs
down to 32

73

72

71

UPPER
FLOORS

52

51

50

49

70

Main
Stairs
down to
Main
Entrance

36

South
Lift

35 40 41 42 43

69a 69

68 37 38 39 44

47 46 45

48

25

A gentle giant

Amitabha Buddha reigned over the Western Paradise. He was gentle and kind. Followers had only to recite his name to be reborn out of lotus buds into his heavenly land. There they could fly with the speed of thought and bathe in clear pools where the water turned warmer or cooler with a wish! Here is a soul in Paradise, born again from a lotus flower.

A temple on wheels

This 'Ratham' was made in India to carry an image of the god Vishnu through the streets on special occasions. It is only a small ratham. Full-size ones were taller than houses.

👁 **Can you see...?**
Vishnu's empty bed
Parasols to keep him cool
Musicians to play for him
Paintings of Vishnu on the pillars

The ratham has been in the Museum for nearly two hundred years. A few years ago the conservators took it all to pieces. They cleaned each part of it with special substances. All the little silk flags were gently washed in water and backed with silk to preserve them.

The ratham is tucked away in a dark corner. This is to avoid damage from light which would fade the cloth. It is not meant to stop you looking at it!

The Judge of Hell

This gruesome-looking character is a Judge of Hell. He and his lady assistant stood in a Chinese temple in the sixteenth century. They were there to remind you that when you died you would be judged according to what you had done on earth. There were lots of different paradises and hells you could be sent to depending on how good or bad you had been.

She holds a thin book with all the good deeds of the world in it. He holds a fat book full of bad deeds. His face is green and fierce as a warning not to misbehave.

Dragons and pots

The Chinese have been making pots out of fine white porcelain for a thousand years. The secret lay in a special type of white stone found in China which was ground to a paste and fired at a high temperature. European potters had great difficulty trying to imitate the porcelain from China which they admired so much.

Rain makes the crops grow, and crops make the land wealthy and happy, so the Emperors adopted the dragon as their special symbol.

You can see plenty of Chinese dragons on pots in the museum.

Here are five of them.

This vase was made over four hundred years ago, when English pots were still being made out of thick coarse clay. It is decorated with six round pictures of dragons. Dragons were thought of as watery rain-bringing creatures.

❓ **One of these dragons comes from the vase on the left Which is it?**
Answer on inside back cover

The Elgin Marbles

The Parthenon was a great Greek temple dedicated to the goddess Athena. It was built over four hundred years before Christ, on a rocky hill called the Acropolis overlooking the city of Athens. The top of the building was decorated all the way round with magnificent marble sculptures.

The triangle-shaped pediment over the East front showed the birth of Athena. At one end the sun-god drove his chariot up out of the sea at dawn. At the other end Selene the goddess of the moon disappeared below the horizon with her chariot and horses.

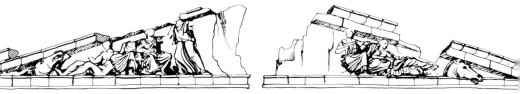

This is Selene's horse, exhausted after a hard night's work.

This is how the sculptures were arranged on the pediment.

Can you spot Selene's horse?

In the nineteenth century Lord Elgin brought some of the marble sculptures from the ruined Parthenon to England and they were put into the British Museum.

Everyday life in Greece

All these things can now be seen in the Greek and Roman Life room in the museum. They would have been familiar to children in Greece about two thousand years ago.

What are they?

ANSWERS

A. A baby's feeding bottle. The writing on it says 'Drink, don't drop!'

B. A wooden writing tablet. The inside panel was covered in wax and children practised their writing on it.

C. An ivory stylus used for writing. Letters were scratched into the wax with the sharp end and 'rubbed out' with the flat end.

D. A baby's rattle, made in the shape of a pig.

E. A spinning top.

F. A chous or little jug given to children at festival-time in Athens. This one shows a child sitting on a potty.

Prizes from the Games

Sporting competitions were very popular in Greece. As well as the great Olympic Games there were many local festivals. Every four years the Great Panathenaic games were held in Athens. The prize for each event was a quantity of olive oil contained in fine painted vases or 'amphorae'.

The other side shows the sport. This prize was won by a champion boxer.

These amphorae always have a picture of the goddess Athena on one side. The inscription says 'I am one of the prizes from Athens'.

Long after the oil ran out the amphorae were valued as fine vases.

When the vase with the boxers on it got broken the owner did not throw it away. He drilled holes in the pieces and clamped them together again with lead staples.

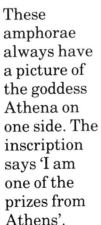 **It has now been mended properly but can you see the old repair holes?**

32

Greek vase painting

Greek vase painters were much admired for their skill. The vases were made of red-brown clay (sometimes coated white). The picture was painted on with liquid clay which went black when it was fired.

Try your hand at vase painting. Your 'vase' can be a brown clay or plastic flower-pot. You can use black enamel or poster paint, or powder paint thickened with **PVA** glue. You can try both the methods used by Greek vase painters.

'Black-figure' painting – (like the vases on the left)

Paint the black outlines of your picture with a fine brush. Fill in the shapes with black paint using a thicker brush. When the paint has dried, scratch out the details with the point of a nail. Paint one of these patterns round the top of your vase.

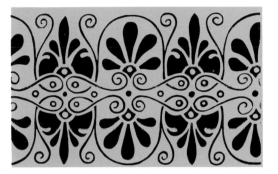

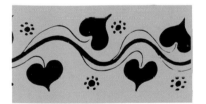

'Red-figure' painting.

Paint the outlines as before but fill in the *background* with black paint. You can then paint in the details on the blank 'red' parts with thin black lines.

Magic carvings

For thousands of years, men have decorated the things they used. Perhaps they hoped that their pictures and carvings would have magic power. Someone in France carved this mammoth out of a reindeer antler about 10,500 BC. It may have been part of a handle for a spear-thrower. It is the oldest work of art on display in the museum.

No-one in the British Museum can solve the mystery of the Folkton drums. Three of these carved chalk drums were found beside the skeleton of a child inside a burial mound in Yorkshire. Nothing quite like them has ever been found anywhere else. What might they have been made for?

👁 **Can you see a carved face with eyes and eyebrows, a nose and a mouth?**

The Folkton drums were made about four thousand years ago, so they are quite new compared with the mammoth!

Treasure trove

When some bits of shiny yellow metal were ploughed up at Snettisham in Norfolk earlier this century, the ploughman thought they were part of an old brass bedstead, and left them by the roadside.

They turned out to be made of gold, the only metal which stays bright and shiny even if buried in the soil.

Later the great Snettisham torc was found nearby. There was a tiny coin inside one of the hollow ends. This showed the torc must have been made by Celtic craftsmen shortly before the Romans arrived.

Torcs were worn by the rich and powerful. A Roman writer said that Queen Boudica, who led a revolt against the Romans, wore one when she rode into battle.

The Snettisham torc weighs more than a kilogram. It is made of gold strands twisted together to make it strong but flexible. It was pulled open and fitted round the neck with the ends in front.

❓ **How many strands of gold in the Snettisham torc? Answer on inside back cover**

The Snettisham gold torcs, like the great Roman treasure hoards also found in East Anglia, were probably buried to keep them safe from enemies. Today they count as treasure trove and belong to the nation.

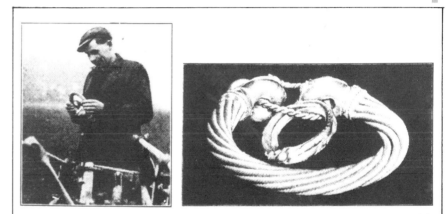

NOTABLE FIND.—Right : An electrum necklet or torque found during the week-end at Snettisham, Norfolk. It weighs 3¼lb. and was described by an archaeologist as probably the finest torque ever found in Britain. It consists of twisted wires with Celtic motifs, chiefly circles and crescents. Mr. Tom Rout, who found the torque, is seen in the left-hand picture.

CELTIC NECKLACE FOUND IN FIELD

Thomas Rout, 22, tractor driver, who is to receive about £120 reward for the 2,000-year-old necklace he found recently while ploughing at Snettisham, Norfolk, yesterday unearthed another gold and silver necklace. He was ploughing the same field 29 yards from where he found the first.

The second necklace, weighing 3¼lb, was described by Mr. Ivan J. Thatcher, the archaeologist, as "probably one of the finest Celtic torcs ever found in Britain." The find has been reported to the police and the district coroner will decide whether another treasure trove inquest is necessary.

INQUEST IS HELD ON TREASURE

By Sunday Dispatch Reporter

VISIONS of Britain before the Roman invasion were conjured up in Hunstanton, Norfolk, Coroner's Court yesterday. Three "hoards" of treasure trove, 2,000 years old, lay before Mr. L. H. Allwood, who held an inquiry under a statute that dates to Plantagenet days.

A special jury of 14 men considered the coins, about the size of a sixpence, believed to be the first minted in Britain, dating from between 85 and 75 B.C., and the gold objects shaped like cornucopias—horns of plenty—ploughed up at Snettisham, near Hunstanton.

The coroner explained that only gold and silver are regarded legally as treasure trove, and it went to the Crown if hidden. If lost or abandoned it need not.

Seized For Crown

The jury held that some gold necklets, found by Raymond Williamson, aged 23, a tractor-driver, on Sir Stephen Green's estate, were treasure trove and had originally been hidden. They were seized for the Crown.

A collection of 70 coins and some Iron Age jewellery in the other two hoards were not treasure — the coroner ordered the jury to ignore small amounts of electrum, a mixture of gold and silver, in them.

Finder of treasure trove, whether it goes to the Crown or not, receives its full market value provided he reports immediately to a competent authority.

The value ? Mr. R. R. Clarke, assistant curator of Norwich Castle Museum, says : "Intrinsically, it is small. From a collector's point of view, it could reach thousands of pounds."

Newspaper cuttings from 1950-51

Roman mosaics

This mosaic picture was found nearly three metres deep beneath Leadenhall Street in London. It was made in the first or second centuries AD as the centre of a floor in a large Roman town house. Mosaic floors were often decorated with pictures of Roman gods and heroes. Here you can see Bacchus, the wine god, riding on a tiger.

Mosaics were made by setting little coloured squares or 'tesserae' of stone, pottery or glass into wet mortar.

Child apprentices began by helping with the simple border patterns which appear over and over again in Roman mosaics. Later they would learn the more complicated art of picture-making.

Large rooms had a central picture with more pictures or patterns around the edge. This mosaic floor came from Hinton St Mary in Dorset.

Make your own mosaic
Draw one of these patterns along a strip of cardboard about 8 centimetres wide. Decide how many colours you need. Collect tesserae of different colours (you can use split peas, kidney beans, lentils, rice, pasta shapes, sunflower or melon seeds, bird seed etc). Put them into

separate containers. Working with one colour at a time, spread a rubber glue like copydex on small sections of the pattern and press the tesserae on carefully.
After pattern-making you may like to try a round picture on a large piece of card!

The Roman Army

The Roman Army invaded Britain in the middle of the first century AD. For the next three hundred years, three or four legions of highly-trained soldiers were kept in Britain. Each legion consisted of 5000 men, and they played a very important part in keeping the country under control.

We know how these legionary soldiers were equipped for fighting because remains of their armour and weapons have been found in many parts of Britain.

Objects in the Roman Britain room show what a legionary soldier looked like.

a dagger with its sheath

a long javelin for throwing at the enemy from a distance

a sword for close-up fighting

a metal helmet for head-protection

Coins and Medals

The British Museum has a collection of coins and medals spanning 2000 years of British history.

Until the seventeenth century all coins were made of gold and silver and they were worth the value of the metal. As money values changed over the centuries, so coins changed in size, and new ones were introduced. In the end silver coins became too small to use. Nowadays our coins are made of base metals and their value no longer depends on their size.

a silver penny:
240 for £1

Medals were often made to commemorate great events. Elizabeth I had this medal struck after the defeat of the Spanish Armada in 1588.

a silver testoon or shilling:
20 for £1

There are about half a million coins in the British Museum altogether. Many of them come from hidden hoards, like these gold coins which were buried in Kent by a Roman soldier. Perhaps he wanted to keep them safe while he was fighting ... but he never came back to collect them again.

a silver crown:
4 for £1

Who are the kings on these three coins? Answer on inside back cover

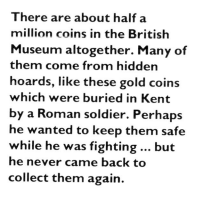

Sutton Hoo ship burial

In the seventh century, after the Romans had left Britain, a huge ship was hauled from the river up a steep slope to a burial field in Suffolk called Sutton Hoo. In this mighty coffin an Anglo-Saxon King was buried. His helmet and weapons, treasure and household equipment were arranged around him ready for the afterlife.

About 1300 years later, archaeologists excavated the mound of earth which had been piled over the King's grave. When the ship was uncovered, the golden treasure still shone brightly, the iron helmet lay in pieces, and the King's bones had disappeared. The wooden ship too had rotted and vanished away, leaving just an imprint in the ground and rows of iron nails.

This magnificent gold belt buckle looks as good as new. Its maker decorated it all over with patterns of twisting creatures.

Can you find two thin snakes with heads like this?

and four snakes with heads like this?

Follow the lines under and over to find their tails. Where is this little biting-beast hiding?

Putting the helmet together again was like doing a jigsaw without a pattern. It had shattered into over five hundred fragments and many were missing. Only the bronze nose and eyebrow pieces had survived intact.

Can you see them in this picture of the fragments?

It took two years to work out what the helmet had looked like, and to fit the pieces together on a plaster base.

This replica of the helmet shows how it looked when it was new over a thousand years ago.

41

Ivory chessmen

The game of Chess has been played all over the world for a thousand years and more. These chessmen were found in a sand-dune on the Isle of Lewis in the Outer Hebrides. There were ninety-three pieces altogether from several different sets. Perhaps they belonged to a merchant who was hoping to sell them.

The chessmen were carved in the twelfth century out of walrus tusk ivory. Some of them were stained dark red to make them different from the white ivory pieces, but this has now worn off.

Chequered chessboards came into use about the time these chessmen were made.

? **Can you name the chessmen in this picture? Answer on inside back cover**

Medieval tiles

The floors of monasteries and cathedrals, palaces and important houses were often paved with coloured tiles during the Middle Ages. These tile patterns came from Rievaulx Abbey in Yorkshire. They were made in the thirteenth century from clay shapes which were fitted together like mosaic.

Tiles were also decorated by stamping patterns onto clay squares and filling in the dips with white clay.

Print a medieval tile pattern

Which of the Rievaulx mosaic tile patterns could you make with these three shapes?

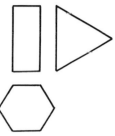

Which of the patterns could you make with these three shapes?

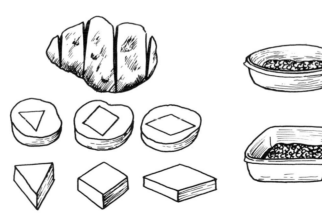

1. Using a sharp knife, cut a large potato into three slices each about 3 centimetres thick. Cut the slices to the shapes of the tiles in your pattern. Match up the lengths of the sides as shown above.

2. Mosaic tiles were usually brown, yellow or green. Choose two colours of poster paint for your print. Line two shallow containers with thin pieces of moist sponge or foam. Put one colour of paint onto each sponge and work it in well.

3. Lay a piece of paper on top of a newspaper. Print your pattern by pressing the tile into the paint and then onto the paper.

A ship-clock

This clock in the shape of a ship was made about four hundred years ago to stand on the Holy Roman Emperor's table. The ship could move along, rocking up and down, with music playing and a cannon firing. It must have given the Emperor a lot of fun!

There are many fine clocks in the museum. You can see some of them working.

Prints and Drawings

The museum has a collection of over two million prints and drawings. Only a few can be displayed at one time, so a new exhibition is organised every few months. The rest are stored in folders and boxes, away from the light which would damage them. They can be studied by students who come to the museum to learn about the work of great artists.

These animals were drawn by Albrecht Dürer nearly five hundred years ago. Later, when he engraved a metal plate to make this printed picture of Adam and Eve in the Garden of Eden, he included them in the background.

Can you spot the rabbit and the elk?
How many other creatures can you see?
Where is the artist's name?

British Museum quiz

(The answers to all these questions can be found in the guide)

Do you remember?

1. Who started the collection which grew into the British Museum?

2. What was the name of the house in which the British Museum began?

3. How many columns were built along the front of the new British Museum building?

4. Where were the animals from the British Museum taken in the 1880s?

About how long ago were these things made? Match each of them to a circle on the time-line.

3000 BC 2000 BC 1000 BC 0 1000 AD

What sort of writing is this?

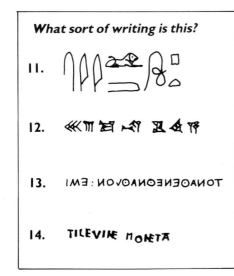

11.

12.

13. ΤΟΝΑΟΕΝΘΟΝΑΟΕΝΘΟΝΟΙ : ΕΜΙ

14. TILEVINE MONETA

The objects in the Museum come from many different countries. The names of the five countries in which these objects were made are hidden in the square. Find each name by moving up, down or across from one letter to the next.

15. *Ratham for Vishnu*
16. *Priestess coffin*
17. *Snettisham torc*
18. *Amphora*
19. *Amitabha Buddha*

Y	G	E	C	E
P	F	E	H	A
T	E	R	I	M
F	N	G	N	D
R	A	L	A	I

Turn to the answers on inside back cover to see how many you got right!

Can you recognise these faces?

21

20

23

22

24

BRITISH COLUMBIA

Museum of Mankind

Explorers in the 18th and 19th centuries brought back interesting things from distant places around the world. Some are unusual, some are everyday things like spears or pots, but they are all interesting because their makers lived in societies where traditions had been passed on for hundreds of years. These objects are collected together in the Museum of Mankind, which is part of the British Museum but housed in a different building near Piccadilly Circus.

This totem pole can still be seen in the main British Museum building as you come down the north-east stairs. It is over eleven metres tall. Once it was part of a large Indian house on the north-west coast of America.

To see everything else you will have to go to the Museum of Mankind in Burlington Gardens. There is plenty there which will interest and amaze you... or may even frighten you!

This mask comes from Ceylon. It represents the Cobra Demon, and was worn by one of the characters in a traditional masked dance.